THE ESSENCE OF MY BEING

Cynthia Snooks-Key

Cynthia Snooks-Key
Snookystyle, LLC
11505 Cherry Tree Crossing Rd
398
Cheltenham, MD 20623-9998

ISBN: 978-1-7360976-0-1

1. Non-Fiction / Poetry / General
2. Fiction / General

Preface

~The Essence of My Being~

I didn't know how or when I would release my spoken word to the world. I didn't know how or when I would allow my most inner thoughts to be heard and shared with others; and then God said "Your when is now!"

Isaiah 43:19 (KJV)

Behold, I will do a new thing; now it shall spring forth; shall ye not know it? I will even make a way in the wilderness, and rivers in the desert.

Dedications

To my Heavenly Father, I praise and thank you for making all this possible. Matthew 18:20 (KJV), For where two or three are gathered together in my name, there I am in the Midst of them.

To my wonderful departed father **"James A. Snooks"**, I miss you so much. Thank you for your wisdom and the love you have poured into me. I remember the first time you read my poems; you were so proud of me. Daddy, you always were my strong tower, always supportive and believing in me.

To my beautiful mother **"Ora Moreland"**, the strongest woman I know. Your love and life lessons have taught me how to survive. Thank you for teaching me how to be independent and responsible, you are my champion. When I was a child you encouraged me to write, a legacy you passed down to me. (Yes, mom writes too.)

To my beautiful niece, my baby, **"Jamyka "Meeki" Forrest"**, our time together is missed, you departed this life way too soon. Your love always made me want to be better. I love and miss you.

Acknowledgements

To my handsome husband and closet friend **"Nate"**. Thank you for loving and believing in me. Your support and encouragement have made this journey possible. I love you with all my heart and soul. My rock, my **"Mr. Key"**; the best is yet to come.

To my daughters, the Snooks girls**: Dr. Qianna "Ki-Ki"**, I love you. You are my greatest creation. Your support throughout this process has been awesome. Thank you for loving me. I am forever your "Pretty Lady" and you are forever mommy's baby. Markita **"Kita-Weta"**, Mommy loves you and my babies **Mariah** and **Logan** (the apples of mom-mom's eye.) **"Daiquan",** I love you, thank you for being their father; you both are great parents. To my Lashawnda **"Le-Le",** you have made my life so exciting and never boring. You keep me laughing. I never know what to expect from you. I love you; never stop being you. My sweet Goddaughter **Ebony,** I love and appreciate you.

To my bestie, **"Duby"** Leslie Stewart-Corneiro, it's been 37 years, you are more than my best friend; you are my sister. Together we have lived life with no complaints or regrets. No grass grew under our feet. Thank you for supporting me and encouraging me to write the many books in my mind's eye. Year after year you would say "Snooks" write the book. Well Bestie, it is done! Thank you for being there for me without conditions. You showed up when others did not. God bless you.

To my brother "**Gerald**", thank you for always keeping it *100*. You bring laughter to my life. I love you. My songbird sister Darlene **"Dolly"**, continue to sing girl. God gave you a voice so use it. To my baby sister Bridget **"Bridgee-Boo"**, you are beautiful inside and out. Keep being you.

Shavon, Shavon, Shavon my **"Little McRae"**, you are my sunshine. Auntie loves you. Continue to believe in yourself, you are a game changer; I am proud of you.

To my Stepdad, James Moreland Sr., **"Pop-Pop"**, you are in heaven now. Your laughter resonates in my mind. Thanks for our long talks. Your *flower* has made it!

To my Stepmom Kathleen Snooks **"Mom Kat"**, thank you for loving me, and encouraging me throughout the years; I love you.

My adopted Aunt "**June Shoemaker**", I miss you, your laughter and our long talks. Your prayers have pushed me through. Thank you so much; I love you.

"Maggie Luzunaris", my sister in Christ, thank you for always being there for me; we have an Agape love.

Thank you, "**Aisha Higgins, Jacqueline Hartsfield, Joyce Baker, Lenora Daniels, Tonya Howard-Williams and Tonya Johnson"**, for contributing to my life, I love you all.

Contents

Chapter 1 - Matters of the Heart

Page

Chapter 2 - It's All About God

Chapter 3 - Urbanely

Chapter 4 - Family

Chapter 5 - Just Sayin

Chapter 1
Matters of the Heart

Proverbs 3:3-4 (NIV)

Let love and faithfulness never
leave you; bind them around your
neck, write them on the tablet of your
heart. Then you will win favor and
a good name in the sight of God and
man.

~And Then It All Fades~

It all goes.
Where does love go when we no longer want it?
Does it all fade?

What does it mean? I am not too sure anymore.
So many closed doors.
Does it all fade?

What is it? Does it really exist?
Does it all fade?

I don't want to feel that good feeling,
especially now, that I am healing.
Does it all fade?

Love, what's love?
I say it's God.

~Appreciations~

Take the time to appreciate all that life has to offer.
Learn to stop raising your voices.
Learn to speak a little softer.

Take the time to tell that someone your inner most
feelings and thoughts.
Tell them in a way they'll understand.
Tell it from the heart.

A close friend was laid to rest. She passed away.
For when she closed her eyes, she did not know that
was her last day.

For we don't know when we will die.
But if today you live, tell that special one you love
them.
Let go of the anger and learn to forgive.

~Believe~

Do I believe in love, sometimes I wonder?
Is it the sound of rain or the roaring thunder?

Is it what makes your heart skip a beat?
Or the feeling of walking light on your feet?

Is it the pain you feel from disappointments?
Or is it a bruise you received that needs a little
ointment?

Some dictionaries define love as affection,
strong liking or even good will.
But do I believe in love?
I wonder still.

It has taken me to the highest mountain,
and dropped me in the lowest pit.
It has brought me joy from different facets,
sometimes I think I conquered it.

So, do I believe in Love?
Oh yes, oh yes, I do.
I believe that from love,
good things will come to you.

But don't get overly confident.
Love has its ups and downs.
I enjoyed love for the most part,
I like having it around.

~Chances~

It took me awhile to understand.
In relationships we all take a chance.

Some couples will make it, some couples won't.
Some couples will try, some couples don't.

In our case it is not the same.
It wasn't me who needed a change.

You built up a wall that was so very high.
What you thought you were ready for
became a surprise.

I dislike you for this and love you the same.
For I have no one but myself to blame.

You said I won't hurt you, now look what you've done,
I've opened my heart and now you want to run.

I didn't want to lose you.
I loved you so very much.
I dream about you often. I miss your touch.

I'll never find another man, not quite as special as
you.
I realized when I lost you,
my love for you was true.

~Distance Memory~

You are a distant memory
Yet so faint
A soft quiet whisper
Familiar yet quaint

There's passion in your eyes
Worth one thousand cries

Of what once was loneliness
To be replaced with
The distant memory of us

~Feelings~

I loved you once and now I don't.
Does that mean my feelings changed?
I see your face and it makes no difference.
For I don't remember your name.

This is not to make you feel good or bad.
You've done that on your own.
And maybe if my wish comes true,
you'll grow old and all alone.

~Friends and Lovers~

It's funny how things occur
It's funny how they change
One day you call me constantly
Then one day you're not the same.

You ask me to understand your reasons
For you they made some sense
For me they meant not one little thing
How could you be so dense?
You said what you've done was for the best
It's a decision that had to be made
Did you consider my feelings
Understanding and all the love that I gave?

I've rethought this over and over again
As each day passes by
And now it seems the whole relationship
Was built on deceit and lies.
How can you love someone and walk away
But not really give them a try
How can you love them and leave them
Without feeling some emotional ties?
I wonder if you have any feelings
Or if you feel real pain
I wonder if you sometimes smile
Or softly speak my name;

I wonder if you remember how
We held each other tight
I wonder if you think about me
In the middle of the night;
I guess it doesn't make any difference
It was your choice to make
I wasn't asked how I felt
You controlled our only fate.
If I could do it differently
What differently would I do?
I would have remained your friend
And not your lover
Only then I'd still have you.

~Hear the Words~

If I could hear the words, I love you,
whispered softly in my ear.
I'd embrace those words forever,
as you gently held me near.

If I could hear the words, I love you,
my heart would skip a beat.
I would dance on nine clouds,
and to heaven I would leap.

If I could hear the words, I love you,
how profound that would be.
Just hearing you say
those sweet words to me.

If I could hear the words, I love you,
sprinkling softly off your lips.
The moon would pass the sun
creating a solar eclipse.

~Holding Back~

You ask me, why do you hold back?
There are so many reasons,
let's go through the stack.
            I tell you I love you,
               but I don't hear it from you.
            While I patiently wait to hear it,
               what's a woman to do?
Can I trust you with my heart?
Are you willing to give me yours?
Can I trust you to love me
without closing doors?
             If I give in like you want;
             will you give in to me too?
             Do you really want me?
             As much as I want you?
I didn't plan to fall in love with you,
 it caught me by surprise.
But the more that we are together,
my feelings I cannot hide.
            Have you ever loved someone so much,
              that they're all that really matters?
             And every time you see their smile,
              your heart beats a pitter patter.
That's how I love you,
and it scares me so much.
I didn't know I could feel this way,
especially from one's touch.
            You whisper in my ear,
             my name you say so sweet.
           As you kiss my neck with your sweet lips,
             you sweep me off my feet.
I'm trying to convey this to you
 without chasing you away.
I want to be in your life forever,
until we're old and gray.
            Thanks for making me breathe again.
             You're not just my lover,
             you're my closet friend.
             So, when you ask me,
            "Why do you hold back";
            Please tell me if you love me,
              for I need to hear that.

~How Soon Will They Come~

How soon will they come
running after you
after you have left?

How soon will they come
to say an apology
that was long ago sought after?

How soon will they come
knowing the mistake was theirs to make
not yours to take?

How soon will they come?

Will they ever learn that staying the same
sometimes means being different?

Will they ever learn that loving someone
doesn't mean running over them?

Will they ever learn that forgiving
doesn't mean staying,
sometimes it is time to move on?

How soon will they come to their senses
and when is too late, really too late?

How soon will they come?

~Hurting~

When we try so hard, why does it keep hurting?
Are we doing something right or wrong?
Why does it keep hurting?

When two become one, that's just what it is.
So, if I am hurting here, I know you are hurting there.

Why can't we stop the pain?
We've tried so hard, please show your heart.
Stop the hurt, stop the pain!
Why do we keep hurting?

I am hurting now.
The more we are in disagreement
the more I feel empty.
Open up! Let me in!
Stop the pain! Show your heart!
Why does it keep hurting?

~I Can't Breathe with You~

I can't breathe with you.
I can't breathe with you.
Each day I suffocate,
exasperated, losing my breath.

I'm dying because
I can't breathe with you.
I can't be me with you.
Because I can't breathe with you.
I'm exasperated, I'm tired,

I'm lonely.
I'm moving.
I've chosen to leave.

~I Wasn't Expecting This~

I wasn't expecting this to be over, but since it is, I
must go.
I wasn't expecting for us to be over, but since we are,
you must go.
I wasn't expecting what you said, but since you did, we
are through.
I wasn't expecting there to be no me and no you.
I wasn't expecting the truths from your heart.
I wasn't expecting that we would end after an
awesome start.
I wasn't expecting too much too soon
I wasn't expecting.......

~I'm Afraid~

I'm afraid of what I feel.
I'm afraid these feelings aren't real.

I'm afraid he can't commit, to me or to him.
I'm afraid he'll hold back and not let me in.

I'm afraid that if I love him, he won't love me back.
I'm afraid to surrender. I'm afraid, I'm afraid.

Yes, I'm afraid. Afraid of the possibilities.
I'm afraid of the humility. I'm afraid.

What I'm afraid of most is being hurt again.
Especially by someone whose become my friend.

I'm afraid of him.
I wish I knew where we stood.
I'm afraid.

~I'm In This Place~

I'm in this place where I thought I found happiness.
Yet, I loss myself. I ceased to exist.
For my desires and my wants died.

They died with what he wanted.
For I felt with my heart and became compromised.

Now I wonder or shall I say ponder,
did I get this right?
It surely doesn't feel that way.

So deep in, should I walk away, or can I?
Not sure, so confused.

This must be a state of mind
feeling so uneasy
and not knowing why.
Can't really put my finger on it,
just trying to figure it out.

In the meantime,.......I'll just **PRAY**!

~I'm Tired~

I'm tired of fighting. It's starting to hurt me inside.
My outward appearance and my looks I can't hide.
The emotions. I'm drained.
What is all this for?

When two lives come together
it's supposed to be for more.
More Love! More Understanding!
More Trust! More Fate!
Two people coming together
and overcoming their mistakes.

It's getting harder by the day.
I'm wondering if I can hang in there?
For lately when we're together,
there's nothing but cold hard stares.

I'm tired.... Of fighting....... **YOU!**

~Is Love an Interpretation~

What is LOVE? Is that a complex question?
I believe it's left up to one's Interpretation.

Some would have you think that love
is this overwhelming everlasting thing.
But what is Love?
When two people vow to love each other.
Is that LOVE?

Do you ask for one's hand in marriage;
and proclaim your love for them,
to be everything they want and need,
just to go behind their back, lie and cheat life a thief?
Is that LOVE?

Do you tell them that your world
wouldn't be the same without them?
But with you in their world the things
you do will make them never forget you.

What is LOVE? Is it ones' own Interpretation?
Can one really, I mean really LOVE?

If a person professes their love to someone,
and tells them they'll do everything they can to keep them.
But yet they lie, by looking the other straight in their eyes.

Is that Love, or is that love compared;
and accepted in ones' own Interpretation?

OK, here's the question:
What is LOVE?

A vow to stand by someone who intern will be there for you;
and to do everything that they can to keep you.
Is that your Interpretation?

But you lie, and you hide, you don't even confide;
What is LOVE?
Please, please tell me.

~Kissed~

When I kissed his face,
it was too late to tell him that I loved him.
As he laid there motionlessly without a word to say,
it was too late to tell him I loved him.
... for he could no longer hear me,
my words touched the air and disappeared in silence,
as though they were never uttered.
It was too late.
He could no longer hear me.

~On My Neck~

He touched me. I quivered. His breath on my neck.
My eyes closed my head back, my heart racing.
So many thoughts, why him wanting me, my soul is so
lost.

I've longed for him, the passion we shared,
so many years so forgotten.
But he's here now, touching me as I quiver.
With his breath on my neck.

Wait! Wait! I must get a grip!
Stay away your too close, this is what I've tried to
forget.
I pull away, he pulls back, into his arms I fell.
Oh, his chest, my face, his embrace!

Its' happening! I can't stop it, and I don't want to.
This yearning, so intense, so erotic I feel ashamed.
But I do it anyway.

Yes, his eyes so beautiful and they are looking at me as
we touch.
I quiver, his breath on my neck, then he kisses me.

I kiss him back, his lips.....
The sweet nectar, how could I forget?

~Once~

Once in a while you get lucky,
fortunate to meet a person of great caliber.
And you wish with all your' might,
that you could make that person happy
for the rest of their life.

Because that person deserves the best out of life.
But circumstances don't permit you to be with them.
The reality of it all and how it ends,
you two continue as friends.

Some won't understand what a perfect package they
are.
And when they treat them wrong, they are missing out
by far.

Good things only come around "ONCE".

~Our Journey~

Our journey could have been the most wonderful
experience that we've ever encountered.

But something went wrong,
you couldn't be strong,
for the both of us.

You wanted to share you with the most of us.
I thought I could get pass it but I cannot.
You said I was all you needed,
but you must have forgot.

You didn't tell her about me, you didn't tell her about us.
You must have forgot because your desire was lust.

I can't trust you now, and I really want too.
But how can you trust someone who as betrayed you.

You can love them with all your heart, you can love them to
the end.
But if you can't trust them with your heart, then love
cannot win.

Our relationship is filled with doubt. Where are you?
Who are you with? Are you really with them?
Is she just a friend?

I don't like feeling like this, but you left me no choice.
You can't even talk to me without raising your voice.

You used to make me happy, but I'm not happy anymore.
So, another chapter is gone,
and now we must close the door.

~Peace of Mind~

I know it sounds bad, but it's really not at all.
These are my feelings in words to circumvent his gall.

He tore it all apart and from the very start.
I put my trust in him, but he didn't want me in.

But no, he didn't say that. What he said was quite
reverse.
I need you; I want you and care for you,
because you I would never hurt.

He was the instrument of my pain.
Even the sound of hearing his name.
Was a fable of an untold story,
but without the fame and the glory?

I mean the hurt, the hurt!
You see the hurt. The hurt from within.
The kind that makes you wants to die
and not come back again.

Like a thief in the night,
he took my heart just to tear it apart.

It didn't take long for his arrogance and ignorance to
show.
He did not know what he wanted,
because he wanted what, he did not know.

~Sentiment~

I wondered why things changed
The children don't say my name
But yet it remains I love them the same.

I may have not been perfect
But remember none of us are
If one gets to live their life this far.

Especially as I
Ignoring the warnings
By giving life a try.

Then you will see it was only thee
Looking for a chance to be forgiven
By my children who didn't love me.

~Roller Coaster of Emotions~

It's hard to picture us here,
When we were there.

Now you greet me with a hug,
What happened to our Love?

What happened to you loving me?
Endlessly.

Till the day you die,
You said that you know, with tears in your eyes.

But now I cry, was it all a lie?
Your betrayal wasn't even justified.

I was a great wife and loved you to the end,
You were no comparison to mere men?

My King, My Othello,
Distinguished upstanding handsome fellow.

~Shutting Me Out~

You're shutting me out, and I don't know what to do,
I tried everything, but you won't let me through.

Maybe it's too hard to talk for it might be about me,
Maybe you need to break these chains and be set free.

We can't continue to live as though it's a lie,
Pretending to be happy, committing mental suicide.

I've given this to God, for that's all I can do,
It's breaking my heart saying goodbye to you.

Yes, I see that's happening right in front of my eyes,
I'm just pretending it's not, and that's no surprise.

Hoping things will change, and the silence will go
away,
But it never gets resolved, and it gets quieter every
day.

For these reasons alone I feel I can't stay,
For my deepest fear within is that one day you'll stray.

~SOMEONE~

You may have someone whom you are waiting for,
but I have no one.

I lay here lonely, night after night,
wondering if it will always be like this or will one day,
I'll find that person to share my life with.

Everyone always has their opinion on the subject.
Such as: Don't worry about it you are not missing
anything,
or I have been married for fifteen years and it is not all
its'
cracked up to be. But the best one is Stay single
you don't know how good you've got it.

Well, here are some good ones for them;
The grass is always greener on the other side,
You don't miss your well until the water runs dry,
and last but not least,
One person's trash is another person's treasure.

~Sunshine and Rain~

You use to be my sunshine, now you are my rain,
You use to be my laughter, now you are my pain.

You said you had it together, and I was what you
want,
But it seems as time goes on, that was just a stunt.

Now I am in my feelings trying to figure out what to
do,
Trying to decide if I should stay or if I should leave
you.

I do love you, and I wish that were enough,
But you don't know what love is, I am asking for too
much.

Life isn't complicated, you make it just that,
You walk around opinionating, like you have all the
facts.

The fact is my dear it's not all about you,
For you give me plenty of good reasons to say I am
through.

Through with your sarcasms and your cynical
reproach,
You act like you have it all together, well baby you
don't.

~The Battle~

Why is it always a battle?
Sometimes I want to ball myself up into a shell
and never come out.
It's always something or someone
trying to make my soul uneasy.

Why is it always a battle?
Constantly,
Constantly,
Constantly, Never giving up.....

Why is it always a battle?

~The Break-Up~

I saw it coming and I turned away,
I did not invite it but it came in to stay.

The quietness, so silent it tipped right in,
Gently pricking like a rose thorn on my soft radiant
skin.

Tormenting me inside, it was ripping me apart,
I was bleeding internally, for it was piercing my heart.

But still in denial I knew it was there,
Looking straight in my eyes with that cold hard stare.

There was nothing left to do but acknowledge the
truth,
There is no more us, No me, and No You.

~To Be Loved~

I want to be loved
I want to be in love
And to love
Is that asking too much?

I was always running from what seemed inevitable
And that was a relationship
But without friendship a relationship is nothing.

You must first realize what you want and go for it
Don't give up when it seems to hard work on it
Because anything worth wanting is worth working on.

So, this is my synopsis on what I want
What do you want?

~To Late~

It's been a while since I've seen your smile
Oh, how I miss you so
It's been a while since I've seen your smile
And how your face once glowed.

We had a bond so tightly knit
No one could tear apart,
At least I thought until that day
You ripped into my heart.

I loved you so, so deeply once
And now you want me back
I can't come back its' too late now
The cards have all been stacked.

~Walked Away~

Why did you walk away?
Knowing one day you would want to go back.

But now you cannot,
The door to that passage is no longer open.

You ruined it, yes it was true love....
All it needed was some nourishment,
Understanding and some patience.

No! No! Not now;
You've done the irreversible,
You moved on,
If you go back, it will hurt the one who now loves you.

So, you stay, wishing you would have never walked
away....

~You and Us~

I look forward to you;
Loving you;
Being with you;
Sharing my life with you.

I look forward to us;
Being together;
Wanting one another;
Needing one another.

In any and every possible way;
I look forward to you and us;
Trying to make it together;
Being there for one another;
Trusting in God,
Because it's all part of His plan.

And you being my man;
(I look forward to YOU and US).

~Your Offerings of Love~

Shall I speak of the romance you have brought alive
inside of me,
while it was the other women you would give your
glance your stare,
your giggles, laughs and care.

Or shall I tell you of the consuming nights that I lay
beside you,
yet you weren't really there.

Shall I tell you about the love I have yet to feel from
you?
The sentiments I thought you felt when you said I Do.

How I embraced you tight throughout the night.
I have had my fill of you to learn,
understand the quench that can never to be fulfilled.
But the only thing in the room,
other than me was the air which was quite still.

What can I offer you of the romance I had with you;
when you were not there?
How can I express the feelings that were between us;
when you never learned how to care?

For from you love was unable to be shared;
It's funny how things manage to work themselves out,
and some say life is unfair.

Your offerings of love, weren't offerings at all.

Chapter 2
It's All About God

Joshua 1:9

Be strong and of a good courage; be not afraid, neither be thou dismayed: for the LORD thy God is with thee whithersoever thou goest.

~A Date with the King~

What a way to end the year, 12/31/08.
I went to church with the King to celebrate the New
Year.

It was awesome, as we drove home,
the King and I talked. Well I did most of the talking.

I thanked Him for all He has done,
and I praised him so much that all I could do was cry.

But then He started telling me about
His promises made to me,
and those tears turned into laughter.

He had me cracking up, it felt wonderful,
He has taken me from Glory to Glory. AMEN

~A Moment in Thought~

Each day I learn something new about me or new about

others.

This past year I have learned more about me,

my surroundings and who I surround myself with.

I am so in tuned with what is right for me and what is

wrong for me;

what I want to hear and what I don't want to hear.

What conversations I privy myself to and the

conversations that I have entertained

(but should have not done so).

I have learned in order to have a peaceful existence

you must first be at peace within oneself.

I've learned that multitudes don't make me, only God does.

I've learned not to lean unto my own understanding,

YES, I've learned.

Have a blessed day,

be inspired and don't forget to Praise Him.

~Born Again~

Do you know where I've been,
Have you seen my sins?
Not just the little ones but the big ones too,
For they are all sins between me and you.

But it's not between you and I,
But our Master in the sky.
He wants us to repent,
And be with him.

Tell the devil he's a liar,
You won't burn in his fire.

Enter into eternity,
Heaven's door is opened wide,
There are Angels soaring in the sky.

Tell the devil he is a liar,
You won't burn in his fire,
Tell him, tell him, just say it,
I've been born again.

~Dearest Friend~

When your loved one passes away,
There are no words to say....

Their charm and their laughter, their life was such a gift,
They are gone but not forgotten, you can truly count on this.

To hear their voice,
Yes; a whisper would do,
To hear them say
"Sweetheart "
Now you know I love you too!

I know you'd love to hear them softly whispering
our name,
I know you'd love to hear their voice
Yet silence still remains.

Such emptiness and loneliness;
Oh Lord, I can't explain,
I am praying dear Father
Please take away the family's pain.

Oh, dear friend, my hearts goes out to you,
Losing someone so Special, know that God needed them too.

You are a dear friend, and your love one was so sweet,
Imagining life without them, I know you are no longer complete.

You'll always have memories and true love from someone who
cared,
You'll always have those quiet moments and the special talks you
shared.

You'll always have the loves of both your lives,
Your lovely grandchildren, the Apples of yours eyes.

There so much more to say but I will leave you with this,
There is none like our God, allow Him to hold you and console
you, Let God handle it.

~Dear Lord~

I see faces and all these places and wonder where I fit in.
I see faces of all these places and now the journey begins.

As I absorb the reality and the passion of my quest,
Wanting to please God not others, while trying to do my best.

So, I'm looking forward not backwards, wanting to get a better view.
Trying to maximize this life experience while getting closer to You.

Lord you have been everything, I mean everything to me.
You have defeated my enemies, and showed your mercy to thee.

When I stumble and fall and my back is against the wall.
It's your name dear Lord, it's your name I call.

Not one time or two times, but seven times more.
You never turned me away, you always answered the door.

I remember crying, so hopelessly through the night,
My tears wouldn't stop flowing; I just couldn't get it right.

But you held me as I laid there feeling doomed without a plight,
You whispered in my ear, "My child it will be alright".

I, your God, will never let you hurt like this again,
Learn to live your life from the beginning,
Because I already know your end.

~Deaths' Angel~

Knowing that death is part of life,
you would think that would make it easier,
But it doesn't.

When that love one passes away
it breaks your heart and all you want to do is cry.

Trying to move on as if things are normal
but they will never be normal again.

A piece is now broken, no words ever spoken
can prepare us for that moment when
DEATHS' Angel comes knocking at the door.

~God's Creation~

I was created to Praise Him!

I was created to Serve Him!

I was created to Love Him!

I was created to Look Like Him!

I was created to Adore Him!

I was created to Need Him!

I was created to Give Myself to Him!

I was created Because Of Him!

I was created By Him!

My Lord......................

~God's Chosen One~

I woke up this morning feeling a certain kind of way,
Then I heard the Lord whisper,
"My child kneel down and pray".

There's a storm coming,
And the enemy can't win,
How many times has he tried;
To destroy you friend?

He'll use your love ones,
Your sisters, brothers,
friends and parents too.
He'll use your children,
Just to destroy you.

'My child do not get comfortable,
For this battle has just begun,
Yet, if you trust in My Word
You know it's already done.

I will make them your foot stool,
so "Child step very high",
Once this battle is over
There will be no need to cry.

But in the meantime,
My child, just do as I say,
I'm sending my Angels
Michael and Gabriel your way.

This battle is real and it must be won,
I have picked you especially,
You're My Chosen One.

~HIM~

I Love the Lord; through the Air
I breathe Him.
When he speaks, I hear Him;
At all times
I praise Him.

He is my Alpha and my Omega
My Beginning and my End.
He is my Confidante, my companion,
He is my closest Friend.

He made my walls of Jericho tumble down,
He stood there beside me
He kept this sinner abound.

I've learned to trust Him
With all that I have.
He gave so much for me
I could never repay the tab.

So, obedience is what I give,
I listen and I obey,
For when this life is over,
I pray to see the Father and Son
In Heaven one day.

~I am God's Vessel~

I am God's vessel,

No matter which way I am positioned

I am still God's vessel.

If you turn me upside down, I am emptied.

If you held me upright, I am full.

You can turn me on either side,

But no matter which way I'm turned

I am still God's vessel.

I am God's Vessel!

~I Saw~

I saw the door to Heaven;
I saw it in the clouds.

I saw the door to Heaven;
It called my name aloud.

I saw the door to Heaven,
What a beautiful site to see.

I saw the door to Heaven;
It was calling aloud to me.

~I'm Lonely~

I'm Lonely Lord,
Just look at the sky it's lonely too.

I look around it's a wonderful life,
And some say death is supposed to be better.

I'm looking forward to it, but I'm scared,
Oh Lord, Oh so scared.

~In My Silence~

In my silence I wrote because I did not have a voice,
and yet that was not my choice.

My insecurities took it away,
keeping things deep inside to avoid the dismay.

Tired of being rejected over and over again;
rejected by family, rejected by friends and especially
men.

He touched me you know where a little girl should not
be touched;
He said hush your mouth baby girl, this is between us.

So, I held it in, year after year,
I saw him, the man, whom I still feared.

He was the one who haunted my sleep,
he violated my innocence; the pain was so deep.

Today it's a memory the pain I've let go;
holding on to it would not allow me to grow.

I open my mouth and words do come out,
giving praise to God, the universe and hallelujah I
shout.

~It's All about God~

I can say it's about me,
but I am merely speaking negativity
Because,
it's all about God!

I can say it's about you, but who are you through and
through,
Because
it's really about God!

I can say it's about them but their just merely men,
made in the image of God!

I can say it's about me, it's about you, it's about them,
but in the end, none of us win if we don't know,
It's all about God!

~Laying in the bed~

As I lay in the bed and I turn my head

and the sun begins to rise,

laying here thinking about nothing in particular

except.......

Why do we have to die?

~Life's Seasons~

You **SPRING** from your mother's womb. (Birth)

Scurrying into the **SUMMER.** (Adolescence)

Gracefully entering **WINTER**. (Maturity)

Until that day you **FALL.** (Death)

~Listening to Voices~

While listening to voices and making choices of things
they do not know,
people give you direction they try to tell you the places
you should go.

Submit your thoughts in prayer to God and the Son
above,
be careful what you share some people do not come
from love.

To be unjust to be untrue is what some people choose
to do,
be careful who you rely on with the endeavors you
pursue.

The Lord is the truth, the light, and the way,
trust Him only,
seek him diligently and always remember to pray.

Rely on Him,
hold on tight to the holy spirit within.

Now before it's all said and done this test is never
through,
God is your creator and He wants to use you.

~My First Love~

My first love, you make me smile so much,
Your presence is so awesome, you have that gentle
touch.

My heart feels so giddy, as I float on the clouds,
I can't describe it, somewhat like thunder, but loud.

You're such a wonder, leaving me wanting more,
You are the Lord my God, the one whom I adore.

I met you when I was young, a child in my youth,
Trying to figure life out and you showed me what to
do.

You took my hand and led the way,
My life with you was no ordinary day.

We walked and talked, we laughed and we cried.
You held me so tight when dear friends died.

When the enemy threw his sphere, you threw
lightening back,
When temptation entered my life, you put me back on
track.

You stayed with me; I didn't deserve such love,
Then finally I realized this love is from above.

My first love, I thank you, for all that you've done,
I know it didn't begin with me; it began with your Son.

~My Soul~

My soul is crying out,
Oh Lord;
For days so long since passed.

My soul is crying out,
Oh Lord;
This ole' life went by so fast.

My soul is crying out,
Oh Lord;
For it needs your delicate touch.

My soul is crying out,
Oh Lord;
For you've blessed me so much!

~Never Give Up~

Don't lose hope and just don't care;

life can be cruel and sometimes unfair.

When things look bleak and so out of touch,

you can count on the Lord, for he loves you so much.

He's more than a conqueror, He's the prince of peace.

Just shout out **Hallelujah** that's a praise to reach.

The truth within is deep down in your soul,

It's the story of giants in old fables told.

The time right now is not to give up.

~The Weights of a Mother~

The weights of a mother just can't be explained;
That's why I call on you "God" your holy name.
As they get older it's supposed to get better;
then you get the Academic dismissal "yes" the college letter.

Then you ask the child what is your destiny,
which way will you go,
They look you straight in your eyes and say "Mom I don't know".

I have no direction; I was taking it day by day,
Isn't that what my Father "our God would say".

Wow, my dear child what's in your head?
If you're going to quote the Father "faith without works is dead".

What do you believe in, do you believe in yourself?
or will you continue with pride, and not ask for help?

You can't hold on, I can't live your life for you,
But I can help you decide which way to go, and what to do.

What happen to your dreams, did you leave them all behind,
You went away to college and loss your mind.

You wouldn't go to class you hardly even studied,
But you made a lot of friends, some terrific hangout buddies.

Are they still at college, I guess they know you're not,
You were there for an education, but somehow you forgot.

You forgot that God is the way, the truth and the light,
And nothing is by coincidence but His Holy might.

Remember how you were brought up, trust in Him alone,
For only through Him can your sins be atoned.

Never forget that you were created for God's glory,
When your book is written, what will be your story?

~There was an Angel in our Midst~

There was an Angel in our midst
Whom we didn't know exist,
She walked through our church doors
To be seen no more.

There was an Angel in our Midst.
Because of her appearance,
Annoyance, and interference;
She was instructed to leave
But she needed to grieve;

There was an Angel in our Midst.
Our Lord is very smart:
He wants to see what's in our Christian hearts.
He sends Angels as a test;
And through our actions
Determines how we are blessed.

There was an Angel in our Midst.
When you see someone, who isn't like you;
Frowning and walking away
Isn't the Christian thing to do.

Smile be polite, show that Jesus is your light.
For that one day could be you,
For you don't know your plight.
And if it were you,
Wouldn't you too want someone to treat you nice.

There was an Angel in our Midst.

~We, Us, Ours~

We have a great life together, wouldn't you agree?
Why mess with perfection, just let it be.

To do right and to know right is God's awesome plan,
one man for one woman and one woman for one man.

When you think about our relationship,
and you begin to pray,
I ask you to open your heart,
and allow God a say.

Allow him to guide you like only He can;
For when I look at you,
you're God's creation,
you're an awesome man.

I believe in what we have, we are truly blessed,
there are things we need to get right,
which is part of this earthly test.

A test of our faith and believing we can,
by doing what God says, by giving us a chance.

To see what can be, in our future at its' best;
by giving it to God
and letting our minds be at rest.

There are others whom have walked our road,
and some whom will do it again,
Trust in God, have faith, for Him you can depend.

~Widows Prayer~

Although you don't know my name,

if you're a wife and you lose your husband you will feel this pain.

I'm a widow and this is my prayer....

I pray that God lifts you up as you feel like your life is down.

I pray that God touches your heart to let you know

that though your spouse is with Him, God will be around.

I pray that God touches your inner spirit; your life will forever be changed.

Chapter 3
Urbanely

Solomon 5:15 (KJV)

His legs are as pillars of marble, set upon sockets of fine gold: his countenance is as Lebanon, excellent as the cedars.

~Black Love~

I'm a Black Woman who loves the Black Man.
Sexy, mysterious, and oh I love His stance.
Some read Harlequin...... but He is my romance.

If you listen very carefully his eyes they do speak,
I love this brother; he is so deep.

His inner most strength sometimes indescribable,
and his passion for life is so desirable.

To change what's been done, to make wrongs right,
To feel free at last is his only plight.

This strong Black Man, I'll adore to the end.
Side by Side, hand in hand, together we'll win.

~Black Pain~

As a black woman I see the pain,
It hurts, I understand, but it still remains.

Our men are treated with such oppression,
When will this change; that is the question?

His struggle has been for some hundred odd years,
He fought, he struggled and he overcame some fears.

But, his fight continues, that I can't understand.
Why don't they leave him alone, **My BLACK MAN.**

~Surrendering to Love~

Surrendering to love, I really want to,
I'm hopelessly, hopelessly trying to figure out what to do.

I want to love you and give you all of my heart,
But will you cherish it and accept it, and not tear it apart?

I want us to last, and not just for today,
I want to share my life with you, and pray you feel the same way.

Stay with me until no Seasons remain,
Sleep with me each night, and in the mornings, whisper my name.

Whisper, "Good Morning Baby", it's me you've been waiting for,
Then enter and take me, as you've done so many times before.

What we share together is like no other's,
The mere thought of our climax, makes my insides shutter.

And when you feel you love me, those words I'll long to hear,
Tell me you want me, when I'm far from you, and not so near.

I found something in you, which I've found in no other,
You've touched my soul; with you I feel covered.

Covered by you and the caring that you give,
You've shared your thoughts, your past, and how you have lived.

How you shared your life with others and it didn't work,
How it messed you up inside, how your heart they truly hurt.

Let us be different, a one of a kind, us two.
Let us be an example of what trusting God can do.

Do I surrender to love, I really want to;
I want to surrender it, surrender it to you.

I'm waiting on you to tell me it's ok,
For me to love you in a very special way.

Waiting for you to whisper these words in my ear,
Sweetheart you can love me, surrender baby,
with me, please have no fear.

~Times Passed~

Times have long since passed..........

We are in Philly where all the people meet
All down Arch, Pine & 6th Street.
Kahoots, 2nd Story, Phoenix and the Ritz.........
That was some 1980's SH...T.

Sista's were dressed,
Brotha's impressed.
Brotha's were fine, Sista's tongues hangin out,
Ooh gurl close ya mouth.

Times long since passed, people hanging out to unwind and having a
good time.
Maybe meet a new friend or meet up with an old one: it was all done in
fun.

Some 20 years later wow, 2001

2001, times have changed we are talking guns, Bang Bang, he's in a
Gang.
Yes, I shot him, just disrespect, didn't really know him, he needed to be
vexed.

It's not my world, I didn't ask to be in it,
I'm a product of what the white man made; I didn't ask to be a slave....

So, now I run my own business, I don't work for the Man.
I sell drugs to my homies and my Fam.

I carry a gun,
because, I am the one.

I paid my dues, I even used.

I am clean at least for now.
If you need me, I'll be around.

Just look for me at my place of business,
I am there day and night,
On the corner of Walnut and Sixty-Ninth.

~True Colors~

I've been on this here earth for some time now,
and some things seem to never change.
Sometimes it's who you know,
and sometimes it's how you play the game.

Or shall I say my skin is not the right color.
I am dark or beautiful tan,
and my bronze is like no other.

But we live in this world where white is right.
Look deep within yourself we both have the same
plight.

To be born and to die,
we have the same fate.
And you'll see it didn't really matter
The Color of My Face.

~Um, Um, Um~

Um, Um, Um, how I love my brothas.......

Um, Um, Um, how I love my brothas........

Chocolate, caramel,
crispy cream 'n' my dreams,
Um, how I love my brothas......

Independent working hard,
taking care of me,
setting my mind free, could this be?

Um, Um, Um,

Woooo, I love my brothas.......

Struggling, falling down,
picks himself up from the ground...
yes, still around.

Dealing, chilling,
sensual, tempting,
caressing the blessings.

Um, Um, Um,
how I love my brothas.......

My brothas like no other;
stand up tall,
against the wall, enjoy it all.

Um, Um, Um...... I love my brothas

~What Lust Taste Like~

I remember what Lust taste like
It's the kiss drip, drip.
Its' the tongue as it enters your mouth;
It's the warmest of the juices,
So succulent so nice,
It's the feeling uncontrollable desires
as your inner parts revive.
That's what lust taste like.
It's the something you want,
had, or couldn't have,
so irresistibly enticing, desires so deep.
That's what lust taste like,
new life breathing into you.

Chapter 4
Family

Colossians 3:13 (NIV)

Bear with each other and forgive one another
if any of you has a grievance against
someone. Forgive as the Lord forgave you.

~Jamyka~

In silence I watched you lay in pain,
while doctors couldn't explain.

First it was your blood,
your kidneys than your heart,
Isn't that where all pain starts?

I watched you slowly slip away,
as I prayed and prayed,
until that day,
When God took you home,
leaving me alone.

In a world without your beauty,
your laughter, and your smile.
My beautiful niece Meeki,
whom I also called my child.
I miss you.

~Eighty Years and Counting~

Dad you sure are blessed,
you are truly one of God's chosen best.

Best father, best husband, best brother, best friend,
you are one of a kind, you are a man among men.

You have a light that shines from heaven above,
you radiate an atmosphere of unconditional love.

You have been blessed with the wisdom of ages untold,
your life has been grander than silver and gold.

Though it hasn't been easy, you pressed your way through,
from a life-threatening automobile accident and aneurism too.

God saved you Dad and we can't thank Him enough,
this life would have been so hard without you, it would have been
tough.

Thanks for sharing your wisdom, your charm and your wit,
thanks for not giving up through life's difficult hits.

Just look around this room, look at the lives you have touched,
the people here today, they love you so much.

I'll end with this scripture, one which touched your heart,
it explains your grey hair and its intricate part.

Proverbs 20:29 *The glory of young men is their strength:*

and the beauty of old men is the grey head.

....and this we can't deny....

I love and salute you Dad **"Mr. James Allan Snooks"**

~Essence of my Being~

What I need is the time to grieve;
to grieve the loss of someone who I loved so dearly.
My Dad.

What I need is for people to stop telling me that it's
alright,
because they don't know what I need;
I need to grieve.

You can't forget a person who you loved forever just
like that,
It's impossible at least so I believe;
I'll always grieve.

I miss him so and I hate he had to go,
and I still grieve.

It's been 6 months and 19 days and still I grieve.
Don't tell me it will get better because it's my heart
that bleeds;
I still grieve.

Grieving doesn't mean I'm depressed,
It means I'm a mess "right now" because right now;

I still grieve for the love I loss;
The mere essence of my being,
My Dad!

~Family~

What's important is FAMILY!
The closeness;
The being together;
The love that you share;
not the falling outs or the difficult times.

Sometimes a bad childhood
will destroy the entire growth
of a functional family with hopes
and dreams and many aspirations,
and make it dysfunctional with criticism,
heartache, and harsh language.

A parents' love to a child is important in its early
years,
this love is what rounds the child
into their perspective part of this universe.

As a parent you can't love with dislike,
you can't build up esteem,
and then knock it down with criticism.

If you do then the child you are neutering
will ultimately grow up with little
or no self-esteem,
no personal growth
and sometimes very confused.

You should talk with your children,
not fight them, you should set good parameters
for them to follow, and understand
their differences and love them just the same.

You should not get angry with them
and stop communicating
because you dislike their views.
That's what a child would do,
you should understand that even
though that is your child,
they are also a person and maybe
now even an adult and
they have their own personal views.

Listen.... We are in a day and age
where parents aren't parents
and children are surely not children,
they are raising themselves;
we must raise them,
and love them and even hold on
when there is nothing left to hold on to.

We are the Parents,
the communicators,
we should open the doors and maybe,
just maybe our children won't close them.

COMMUNICATE!!!!

~Husband, Father, Dad, Pop-Pop~

Husband, Father Dad, Pop-pop, oh what a Friend,
It saddens us on this day to know it had to end.

But we all must take this path one day,
So, live this life for God and always remember to pray.

Earth is the beginning for our lives with God above,
I imagine dad with wings flying like a dove.

James Moreland, our dad
Your laughter filled a room, your charm, most impressed,
Now let me take a moment to talk about the way you dressed.

Your suits were sharp, no one could compare,
When you walked out the door everybody stared.

They'd say there's Mr. Moreland can't you see,
Where is he going looking dapper as can be?

Stacey Adams on his feet, his sophisticated hats,
This was his normal attire,
Sitting on the porch just to chat.

Let's not forget about the shades,
he wore on his face,
And no matter what the occasion
they never seemed out of place.

I loved to see you walk,
your stance strong and bold,
I remember how we talked and every story you told,
some old ones, some new ones,
some just to teach a lesson,
but what I learned from you,
I consider truly a blessing.

For knowing you enriched our lives,
in ways we can't explain,
and now that you're gone,
our lives will never be the same.

~DAUGHTER~

I watch my daughter in her innocence,
and I wonder where it will all go.

For I like her young and inexperienced,
the adult part I just don't know.

I see my 15-year-old child growing up so fast;
I just want time to stop; I want this moment to last.

Has she grown, I hoped it would be slow,
oh, lord tell me where did all that time go?

I don't care if she's 15 times 3,
she'll still be my baby girl to me.

~My Father, My Friend~

Though miles keep us so far apart,
I want you to know you are here in my heart.

There's not a day that goes by that I don't think of
you,
You're my Father, my Friend, the Man I look up to.

When you're feeling alone, just plain down and out,
Remember I love you, and there's never a doubt!

My present to you is very unique,
Not gold, diamonds or anything sweet.

It's the love of life, that will never change,
It's a gift from God, bless his Holy name.

I love you, your daughter

~My Mother~

I remember the flower you made me and what lead to that event;
I remember you shaking and trembling,
and straight to the hospital we went.

You weren't yourself that day, you weren't even alert,
and when I looked into your eyes all I saw was pain and hurt.

You are such a strong mother with so much strength,
what I didn't see was how deeply
the pain you were feeling within.

Life for you was never easy being raised by others as a child,
you thought about your biological parents
every once and a while.

When your marriage to dad didn't work
you were left to do it alone,
you kept a roof over our heads
and made our house a home.

Raising four children on your own was really, really rough,
you had to work two or more jobs I know that had to be tough.

You laughed when you wanted to cry,
and you cried when you wanted to laugh,
you took on this thing called motherhood and all its menial tasks.

Your sacrifice is not forgotten I know we were truly blessed,
thank you for not giving up on us four; we could sometimes be a
mess.

We only get one mother,
and you're the mother for me.
Thank you, mom, Ora Moreland
the first limb on my family tree.

~Ode' To Thee~

You are Seventeen and it's time to
Grow up,
Hush up, and
Listen up.

You want advice only when it benefits you,
And when it doesn't,
"You are misunderstood.

Parents don't know everything,
but they do know they love you.
They won't mislead you,
and they only want to protect you.

So, listen up,
Hush up, and
Grow up....

Then and only then once you've thought it through....

Stand tall
Hold your head high
And.... Speak Up!

You'll be surprised who'd listen, it might be me.

Chapter 5
Just Sayin

Isaiah 55:11 (KJV)

So shall my word be that goeth forth out of my mouth: it shall not return unto me void, but it shall accomplish that which I please, and it shall prosper in the thing whereto I sent it.

~Folks~

I'm not like some folk,

Well, maybe a few folks,

No, I'm just plain folk,

Yeah, that's me.

~Friends~

Friends disagree;
but yet they are still friends.

Friends don't always see eye to eye;
and when they question why;
they are still friends.

Friends can seek just as well as find;
what intrigues them about each other's minds.

Friends are there not just when it counts but,
even when it doesn't.

Friends love you,
even when they don't understand you.
Yet they remain friends.

Being a friend doesn't mean leading or following,
asking or telling,
but being there when it counts.

Thanks for being a friend.

~Goodbye~

What's so "good" about Good Bye?
Good means something special something nice;
Bye means, just that,
see you later or maybe not.

So, what's up with Good Bye?

There is no such thing,
not unless you phrase it differently such as;
I found a good buy at the store the other day,
but not I love you but I must say Good Bye,
just say "bye"; there's nothing good about that!

So, don't say Good Bye,
say I'll see you later or just say "later".

~I Don't Fit In~

I am sitting here, in this space,
but I don't fit in.

I've tried, believe me....

They converse but yet I hear nothing,
at least nothing that pertains to me,
or anything, which I seem familiar with.

Then they laugh....

And expect me to join in, but I don't.
I am sitting here in this space where I don't fit in.

~I Love My Fifties~

I don't want to pop it, drop it, or even flop it.
If you're over fifty and still doing that,
please just stop it.

Yes, that existed once,
but it doesn't exist now.
That is not how a woman
of God gets down.

This time of your life should be
filled with peace and relaxation,
...and...
when it's time to avoid nonsense
there should be no hesitation.

So, sit yourself down and stop all that mess,
Be that woman of God; and that you can attest.

~I Miss You~

I was driving today and gazed up at the clouds,

they were so beautiful,

they looked like big white mountain;

but there was this one little cloud sitting all by itself,

(it missed its' mountain).

So close but yet so far.

~I'm Not Ready~

I am at a place where solitude is my only comfort.

If I shall utter a word, then the silence will be broken.

I'm not ready!!!!

No! I'm not ready to handle it.

~Just Begun~

(We've only just begun)
Oh yeah it sounds like a song,
but really in my heart I know I was wrong.

I apologize for my sincerity is true.
It would really hurt me to lose a friend like you.

Since that night nothing has been the same.
But I have no one but myself to blame.

So, let's start all over, I mean like we were before.
They're not many friends like you around anymore.

~My Friend~

If I were to get married again,
I'd like to marry my friend.

Hanging out, laughing or even dancing;
cuddling and holding and a lot of romancing.

Taking long walks would also be enjoyable,
yes, I'm a romantic, I know, I'm incurable.

I want to look at him and know I chose right,
not wondering if I'd made a mistake
by ignoring my insight.

I'd love him with all of my heart,
not allowing anything or anyone to tear us apart.

He would call me during the day and even answer his
phone,
he wouldn't have a nonchalant attitude," Like leave
me alone."

A companion would be nice but,
ONLY if I were old,
at least that's what senior's say,
or least I am told.

If I were to get married again,
I'd marry my friend.

~Metaphor~

You gave me four wonderful years

and now I must leave you.

There's nothing left except space.

Sometimes I wonder if you hear my voice

bouncing off the walls, O' I miss you!

My Apartment!!!!

~No More~

There's a wall of silence, and your name is chiseled on
it.

There's a bed at night which your back is turned.

There's a question asked,
and your response is the same.

Silence

When I ask what's wrong,
the reply is too many thoughts.

No More – sleeping and not holding me;
No More - turning your back on me;
No More – Isolating me;
No More;
No More;
No More!

I am not your enemy.

~Oh My~

Oh my!
I heard about your eye.
I thought I would just cry.
It should have been a stye.

I was very concerned,
to what I had learned.
If you can't win,
make sure they're your twin.

You know the old saying
when you are fighting not playing,
and "Eye" for and "Eye"
and a "Two for a Two'.

~The Ingredients of our Friendship~

½ Cup of Generosity
¾ Cup of Understanding
1 Cup of Love
A dash of Tolerance
And a Life Time of Trust.

You mix 1 Cup of Love
and ¾ cup of understanding until they boil.
Let them simmer down for 5 minutes
then add a dash of tolerance and "CHILL" overnight.
Garnish with Generosity and
Life Time of Trust and think of me.

~Words~

Words that have been said,

which should have never been spoken;

will forever be chiseled into that love one's heart.

And when tried to erase,

no words can replace the mere

existence of which was already said.

www.ingramcontent.com/pod-product-compliance
Lightning Source LLC
Chambersburg PA
CBHW071101090426
42737CB00013B/2414